Frog
Features

Sharon Callen

Frogs have their own creature features.

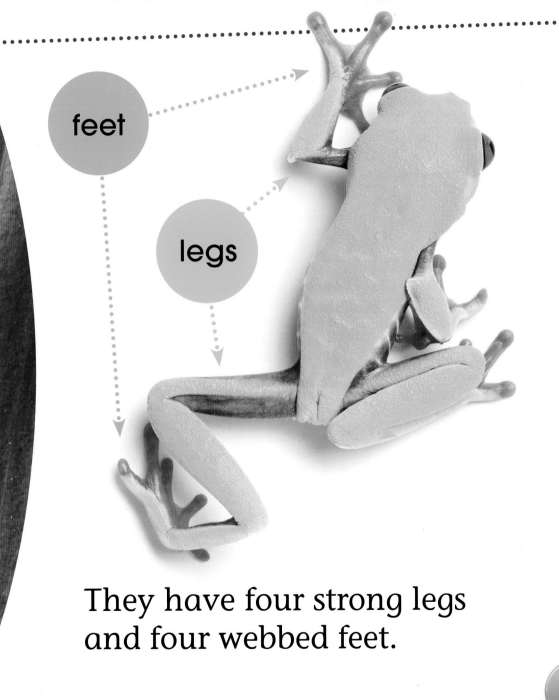

feet

legs

They have four strong legs
and four webbed feet.

eyes

skin

Frogs have two big eyes
and smooth skin.

4

tongue

A frog has a long sticky tongue.

Frogs can jump.

It's a Fact

Frogs can jump
more than three feet.

Frog Features

legs	4
feet	4
tongue	sticky
skin	smooth